The Worst Football Team 3: Spiders

Martin Smith

Illustrated by

Philip Knibbs

Martin Smith

ISBN: 978-1-7395373-3-3

For Tim, the specialist

defence coach

Contents

Acknowledgements

1. We go again   1

2. Monday night   7

3. Spider Fan   14

4. Tactics … again   19

5. Setting up   30

6. Not setting up   36

7. Photo   42

8. Secret weapon   51

9.   Kick-off   56

10. Spider saviour   63

11. Help   76

12. Peace   84

13. Loose leopard   91

14. Second half   96

15. Fog dood   112

About the author

About the illustrator

Copyright

Acknowledgements

Football comes in all shapes and sizes.

At the U7s level, soccer is seen at its purest.

Lane FC Meerkats are certainly not the best team, but they are special because football brings people together.

It's the Beautiful Game, after all.

Those children will remember these adventures for the rest of their lives.

This is the third book of the Worst Football Team series –

and it's been more popular than I ever imagined.

Phil Knibbs' wizardry brought the Meerkats to life brilliantly, while Mark Newnham created the eye-catching cover.

Alan Poole kindly took time out of a very busy social schedule to provide the copy edit before grammar king Richard Wayte finished the task with the usual proofreading masterclass.

Finally, thank you to you for reading.

Oh, and always, always believe.

1. WE GO AGAIN

Welcome back.

I'm a little surprised you've turned up, to be honest.

Meerkats are not doing very well, are they?

Let's review the team's recent results and performances.

Games: two.

Wins: zero.

Draws: zero.

Defeats: one (although it should be two).

Games abandoned: one.

Goals scored: one miskick by Dazza.

Goals conceded: too many to count. Hang on, I could probably count them, but it would take a long time.

Let's say … LOADS.

The number of players refusing to play: one (Stevie).

Brendan and Bolo are hiding after a combination of wee and bogeys got the last game cancelled.

JP – the coach of the Under-15s and nicknamed King Buffalo by the Meerkats – is still on the warpath.

Oops.

We promised Coach Mark we would NEVER mention the incident involving JP, the chilli bogey cakes and the bottle of wee again.

It is too horrible to even think about.

JP has fully recovered now, thankfully

The ref is another matter. He has not been seen since, although Coach

Mark did leave some chocolates – fully wrapped – on his doorstep as an apology.

Coach Mark has moved training to Monday nights. This is sensible because they no longer have to face JP or his team of Under-15 buffalos during training.

The good news is that Dazza has recovered from food poisoning and is back in training.

But there's bad news too.

Stevie is still unhappy with Coach Mark about lizards. I would explain it, but Stevie gets upset if it is mentioned.

This is tricky.

Meerkats need seven players to play matches. Without Stevie, they have six.

Coach Mark has pleaded with Stevie.

Hildy has tried.

Pellie too.

Stevie will only come back if he – and every spider in the world – gets a full apology from Coach Mark.

Coach Mark is not happy with this idea.

He does not want to apologise for liking lizards. He used to own one.

But Meerkats REALLY need Stevie.

They need a sub.

Dazza can only play for half a game, perhaps less.

Much less, probably.

They must have seven players.

And that means getting Stevie to play again.

And an apology.

To Stevie and the spiders.

Let's go and join them, shall we?

2. MONDAY NIGHT

Coach Mark stands in front of the Meerkats.

It is the start of training.

Everyone is there.

Stevie hangs back, holding his spider book while giving Coach Mark evil looks.

Coach Mark ignores Stevie's death stares.

"Hi gang. Welcome back.

"Dazza, I hope you're feeling better?"

Dazza, wearing the latest England tracksuit, missed the last game after scoffing more food in a single afternoon than most people eat in a week.

Today the Meerkats' leading scorer – with one goal – is back.

Sipping a bottle of fizzy drink, Dazza gives a thumbs-up.

Coach Mark does not allow his team to drink pop at training, but he does not say anything.

There are bigger things tonight.

Coach Mark is honest.

"We did not play well last week."

This sentence does not go down well.

"The ref was a FAKER!" Hildy looks ready to explode.

"He was a CHEAT!" Pellie agrees, as always.

"He RUINED the game," wails Dribbler.

Bolo and Brendan remain quiet. Both turn red.

Coach Mark shakes his head.

"He had to have three stitches in his leg because of you, Hildy."

Hildy pulls a face: "It was a great tackle."

Dribbler chips in: "He was a DIVER."

Dazza stops drinking.

"The ref was in a car? Wow. The club never allow cars on the pitch. I missed all the fun!"

Hildy shakes her head.

"No, not a driver. A DIVER."

Dazza looks even more impressed: "Wow. That's AMAZING. Did he go to the Olympics?"

No one answers.

Darren continues: "Hang on. You lot played a match next to a swimming pool … and asked some chap on the diving board to be the ref? That's insane."

Pellie touches Dazza's arm: "Are you OK?"

Dazza looks confused.

"Yes, I'm fine. What was wrong with the diver referee?"

Dribbler frowns: "No, dude. He

wasn't a diver like that. You know, he faked an injury. He wanted to get home early rather than finish our match."

Coach Mark is already fed up with the conversation.

He checks his watch.

There are still 58 minutes and 30 seconds until training ends.

That is a LONG time.

He takes a deep breath.

"That is not true. That fella is a good egg. He has refereed games for Lane FC for 20 years. He told me he will NEVER referee one of our games again."

Hildy and Pellie smile.

They do not like that ref.

Brendan picks his nose.

Bolo's hands go up his sleeves to keep warm.

Coach Mark stops talking about the ref.

He looks over the top of the Meerkats' heads towards Stevie.

He clears his throat. It is time.

"As you can see, Stevie has joined us again."

Everyone turns towards Stevie, who has the usual red bow tie around his head.

He looks FURIOUS.

Hildy smiles.

She thinks Angry Stevie is the best.

Coach Mark continues: "Stevie, I would like to apologise. I made a bad mistake."

Pellie's hand shoots into the air.

"What did you do?"

Coach Mark sighs.

"I – accidentally – did something that upset him. It was silly and I regret it."

Dazza screws the top on his bottle of pop.

"You haven't upset me."

No one understands why Dazza has said this.

Pellie put her arms around Dazza.

"Are you certain you're feeling OK?"

Dazza frowns. His tummy does feel a little odd.

Everyone's attention turns back to Stevie.

Stevie's lips are so thin you can barely see them.

He points at Coach Mark, eyes bulging, and roars: "HE HATES SPIDERS!"

Everyone stops.

Silence.

This is serious.

The Meerkats' eyes return to Coach Mark.

How could Coach Mark do this to Stevie?

3. SPIDER FAN

Dribbler gasps.

Pellie's jaw drops.

Bolo's eyebrows go as high as they can.

Brendan stops pulling out a giant bogey. It dangles from his left nostril.

Dazza rubs his tummy.

Hildy has turned bright red.

"Coach Mark, how could you?"

Hildy is usually Coach Mark's biggest fan, but this is a step too far.

"No wonder Stevie has not been playing. This is disgraceful, Coach Mark," says Pellie, who appears to enjoy arguing more than training.

Dribbler wails: "You've always been so kind, Coach Mark. Why are you trying to upset Stevie?"

Things are getting difficult.

Coach Mark speaks gently: "This is all a big mistake.

"I … said I liked lizards. And I am deeply sorry."

"Lizards?" say Hildy and Pellie together.

"Lizards?" says Dribbler, rubbing his head.

"Lizards?" says Brendan, picking and flicking the swinging bogey.

They look at Coach Mark and Stevie.

And back to Coach Mark.

Coach Mark. "Yes. Lizards. I am very sorry.

"I really want Stevie to come back and join us. We need him."

Everyone stares at Stevie, who continues to glare at Coach Mark.

Angry Stevie looks like a firework. The fuse has been lit and a big explosion is coming at any moment.

Hildy jumps from one foot to another. She can't wait.

Dribbler is bored. He looks towards the footballs. He likes training.

Brendan has finally captured the ultimate bogey from his nose. What a day.

Dazza breaks the silence.

He says: "Lizards?"

The team groans.

To everyone's surprise, Stevie stops glaring at Coach Mark.

He turns to Dazza … and almost smiles.

Hildy pulls a face. She LOVES Angry Stevie but Normal Stevie is nowhere near as much fun.

Ignoring Hildy, Stevie takes a step forward and – incredibly – holds his precious book about spiders towards Dazza.

"Yeah, lizards eat spiders. It's all in here. Take a look."

Dazza puts down the bottle and takes the book, handling it carefully.

He does not want to upset Stevie either.

The boys study the page together.

The rest of the team watch nearby, confused.

Coach Mark breathes a massive sigh of relief.

Stevie is back.

Meerkats are a team once more.

4. TACTICS AGAIN

Coach Mark has a whiteboard set up.

It is a day before the third game of Meerkats' season.

But this match is different.

It is a game where Meerkats have a chance of scoring.

Yes, you've read that right.

Trundle FC are TERRIBLE.

Of course, they are not as awful as Meerkats, but still rubbish.

Everyone beats them.

Tomorrow, Meerkats will play them at home.

It is exciting.

Meerkats have never won a game.

This is their chance.

So they have to take it seriously.

The Meerkats are having a tactics meeting.

This is the team's second attempt at understanding Coach Mark's tactics.

The first was a disaster.

Once again, the gang is confused – why does Coach Mark want to talk about sweets?

How is that going to help them play better?

The players are sitting in front of the whiteboard.

Dazza has Stevie's book about spiders in his lap.

Stevie holds another copy of the same book, but his looks newer with a brighter cover.

They sit together, beaming with joy.

Hildy is scowling. Normal Stevie is rubbish. Happy Stevie is even worse.

She misses Angry Stevie.

After the chilli booger cake incident, Bolo keeps checking the clubhouse, worried about JP.

Coach Mark begins: "Thank you for coming today, Meerkats.

"I need your concentration because tomorrow is a big game. Can you do that?"

Pellie and Hildy nod eagerly.

Dazza whispers: "Do what?"

Bolo responds: "Concentrate!"

Dazza does exactly as Coach Mark requests – and concentrates on Stevie's book about spiders.

It is brilliant.

Coach Mark continues: "Gang, you have been brilliant so far. I'm so proud of you, but you can get better."

Excited chatter breaks out among the team.

Dribbler does a little dance.

Hildy and Pellie high-five.

Stevie keeps reading.

So does Dazza.

Coach Mark claps.

"I'm thrilled you're excited."

Pellie interrupts.

"What colour are we wearing?"

Bolo looks at her.

"You're wearing white shorts and a red Christmas jumper, which is weird. So red and white."

Stevie and Dazza stop reading and study Pellie's clothes.

Bolo is correct. Pellie is wearing a Christmas jumper.

Hildy scowls at Bolo.

"Pells can wear what she wants!"

Pellie starts crying.

"Bolo HATES Christmas!" she wails.

A fresh voice speaks.

"He did not say that. Bolo said it is weird that you're wearing a Christmas jumper. That's all."

Brendan rarely says anything.

Everyone looks at him suspiciously.

This is odd.

Coach Mark says gently: "We'll be wearing our blue kit as normal."

Pellie blows her nose.

"How could you make us wear that again? I've dreamed about getting a yellow kit. And now you've RUINED it," she says icily.

Dribbler laughs.

"We've only been playing games for two weeks. Get a grip, Drama Llama."

Everyone gasps.

This is the worst thing anyone in Meerkats has EVER said. If you forget about lizards.

Pellie goes bright red.

Hildy throws herself at Dribbler.

She misses and crashes into Dazza, knocking the spider book off his lap.

Before anyone else can react, Coach Mark scoops up the book and puts it on the table.

Thankfully, Stevie is so engrossed with reading he hasn't noticed the kerfuffle.

Coach Mark breathes a sigh of relief. In one smooth move, he picks Hildy up and places her next to Pellie.

Coach Mark tries again.

"Meerkats, we need to concentrate. Our kit is blue. We don't buy a new kit every game."

Pellie is cross. She wants a yellow kit.

Coach Mark tries to calm her down: "Your goalkeeper top is yellow, Pellie. It's the others who wear blue."

Pellie had forgotten this.

She keeps quiet.

Coach Mark continues: "Team, we don't have long left. We need to talk about how we're going to play."

Dribbler's hand goes up this time.

"Yes, Dribbler?"

"Will our new kits have our names on the back?"

Hildy nods: "Pellie has already asked about new kits. Weren't you listening?"

Dribbler does not reply.

He hadn't been listening.

And the blank faces on the rest of the team show they weren't listening either.

Coach Mark speaks slowly.

"The shirts don't have your names

on them because THERE ARE NO NEW KITS. Hildy is right, we have covered this."

Hildy smiles. She likes to be right.

Pellie smiles because her bestie is happy.

Coach Mark tries a final time: "We have blue kits. It is Brendan's turn to wash the kits this week.

"He will bring them on Saturday morning before the game. They WILL NOT have names on the back. Is that clear?"

Bolo shrugs.

"I know everyone's name anyway."

Hildy snorts: "Do you?"

Bolo scowls: "Yes. Easy."

Dazza joins in.

"Yeah, we all know."

Hildy looks around.

"Go on then, what's Dribbler's name then?"

Silence.

Bolo scratches his chin.

Dazza loses interest. He returns to the spider book.

Bolo finally replies: "Dribbler?"

Dribbler nods.

"Correct. Well done, Bolo."

Hildy looks cross. Dribbler's real name is not Dribbler.

"That's cheating, it's not…."

She stops talking as the clubhouse door swings open.

Apart from Stevie, everyone turns to see the new arrival.

Bolo and Brendan go white.

JP – manager of the U15s and nicknamed King Buffalo by the Meerkats – stands in the doorway.

The same JP who ate a chilli bogey cake and then drank a bottle of Bolo's wee by accident.

He is the Meerkats' biggest enemy.

Coach Mark breaks the silence: "Session over, gang. I'll see you for the match tomorrow."

The Meerkats flee, leaving Coach Mark standing next to the tactics board that has not been touched.

5. SETTING UP

Coach Mark arrives early for the Meerkats' big match against Trundle FC.

Things have started badly.

Brendan and his parents turned up as Coach Mark unlocked the car park gates.

Sadly, they had forgotten the team kits, so they dashed home to retrieve them.

Coach Mark tried to forget the missing kits.

Today is important.

Trundle FC Under-7s are pretty awful.

Coach Mark knows this. It is a massive chance for Meerkats not to lose by a gazillion goals.

He has lots of things he must prepare for the game.

First, the toilets have to be opened.

The plastic goals must be made. They're like a jigsaw for grown-ups.

Corner flags need to be stabbed into the ground.

And a weird rope barrier must be erected to prevent naughty parents from invading the pitch.

Carrying balls and his trusty kit bag, Coach Mark stops at the Lane FC pitch.

One of the goals is already made up.

Coach Mark picks up a note – with odd-looking writing – attached to the goal.

It says:

"Coach Mark, we used this goal for training last night so we've left it up for

you! Cheers, Bill."

Coach Bill runs the Under-8s team and Coach Mark thinks Coach Bill is an absolute legend.

Today is going to be a great day, he decides.

It's one less thing to do.

"Morning, Coach Mark!"

Coach Mark jumps.

Dazza is wearing a perfectly ironed tracksuit and carrying several water bottles.

Despite being before 8.30am, he's eating a massive sandwich with chicken nuggets and pasta inside it.

Coach Mark ignores the food. Instead, he checks his watch.

Dazza is 34 minutes early for warm-up.

And 64 minutes early for the game.

Coach Mark smiles.

"Morning, Dazza. Ready for the

big game?"

Dazza's mouth is full again.

He tries to speak but can't, so he nods instead.

Coach Mark replies for him: "Great. Once you've finished your … breakfast, grab a ball and begin warming up."

Dazza nods once more, chewing merrily on the nugget pasta breakfast.

Coach Mark tries not to look at the sandwich. He begins to walk to the other end of the pitch.

The other goal needs to be set up before Trundle FC U7s arrive.

He has work to do.

Coach Mark has put together one post when an almighty cry comes from behind him.

It is so loud there can only be one answer: JP has unexpectedly arrived.

But, when Coach Mark turns

around, there is no sign of the U15s coach, which is the good news.

The bad news is that Dazza is running towards him, spitting bits of the sandwich as he shouts.

By the time Dazza reaches Coach Mark, he can't talk and looks deathly pale.

Dollops of chicken nuggets hang off his chin, and pasta twirls sit in his hair.

Coach Mark is alarmed.

They are the only two on the field. He is unsure what on earth could have caused such a reaction.

After several moments of deep breathing, colour returns to Dazza's cheeks.

Coach Mark squats beside him.

He says kindly: "Dazza, breathe. That's it. What has caused this?"

Dazza's eyes grow large.

He begins to panic.

His breathing goes funny again.

He points toward the goal that's been sitting outside all night.

One word comes out of his trembling lips.

"SPIDER!"

6. NOT SETTING UP

Coach Mark is standing in front of the goal.

Dazza is correct.

There is a spider.

It is big.

And hairy.

Coach Mark edges closer to get a better view.

Dazza screams: "Don't get too close! It'll KILL us!"

The spider doesn't move.

Coach Mark shakes his head.

"Don't be daft, Dazza."

He can see it clearly now.

Overnight, the spider has made a web between the crossbar and the goalpost in one of the corners.

Small droplets of water hang from the spider's silk.

Coach Mark gets closer.

The spider is sitting in the centre of the web.

Waiting.

It is … HUGE … with long legs. Coach Mark knows nothing about spiders. Yet this is bad.

Coach Mark does not know how Stevie will react to this shocking discovery.

The team cannot afford to be without a sub again. Not today.

Dazza whispers: "Is it poisonous?"

Coach Mark snorts: "Of course not."

He has no idea whether this is true.

Dazza looks a little happier.

"Will it bite us?"

"Don't be silly."

Once again, Coach Mark is bluffing.

He has no clue about spiders. He likes lizards, not spiders, although he can no longer admit that.

He does what all adults do when they don't know what they're talking about. He changes the subject.

"Hang on, I thought you'd read all about them in Stevie's book?"

Dazza blushes: "I've only read four pages. There's A LOT of words and hardly any pictures.

"What are we going to do?"

It is an excellent question.

Coach Mark's training did not cover spider issues.

Yet spiders seem to give him more footballing headaches than anything else.

Coach Mark sighs.

Time is running out. In the distance, he can see Trom Revol, coach of Trundle U7s, unpacking his car. There is so much to do.

Coach Mark makes a decision.

"We'll have to move it."

Dazza steps back. "I'm not going anywhere near it. I hate spiders.

"I'm giving Stevie his book back. I'm not moving it.

"Not a chance."

A new voice says: "What are we moving?"

Coach Mark and Dazza jump.

They thought they were alone.

WRONG.

Hildy is standing nearby with Pellie a few metres behind her.

Both are beaming with smiles.

And they are spotless.

It won't last.

Hildy will be mud-splattered before the end of the warm-up.

But that can wait. He needs to move the spider but, before he can tell the girls this, Dazza jumps in first.

"There's a KILLER spider living in the goal and Coach Mark wants me to wrestle it and squash it."

Coach Mark is lost for words.

Hildy and Pellie are HORRIFIED.

Pellie says: "Coach Mark, you cannot do that. The poor little thing."

Hildy adds: "Imagine how Stevie will feel if he finds out you've booted a spider out of its home."

Coach Mark does not have time. His brain is working hard. Then he realizes that the answer is obvious.

It is staring him in the face. And it may just change EVERYTHING for the Meerkats.

7. PHOTO

Coach Mark has got the other goal up.

This means that the Meerkats have not had a warm-up.

But today is different.

Coach Mark has the secret weapon.

Apart from Brendan, the entire team is there.

Trundle FC have been warming up for 20 minutes.

Meerkats are talking about Poggo, the team's sponsor. Coach Mark tells the team that the company makes delicious cabbage.

No one has heard of them.

Pellie frowns.

"Poggo? It sounds like…."

"Piggo?" Bolo tries.

"That's not a word," replies Pellie.

"Bobo? There's a girl in my class called that," announces Dribbler.

Dazza clicks his fingers. "Togo? Isn't that what badgers wear?"

This makes no sense to anyone.

No one replies to Dazza, who is finishing the remains of his pasta sandwich.

Pellie ignores the boys' ridiculous suggestions.

Stevie replies quietly: "Dodo is a bird that can't fly, but they are not around anymore because of … stuff."

No one has mentioned a dodo, but the rest of the team does not want to disagree with Stevie.

"I'm hungry," says Dazza, still licking his fingers after the last bite of the sandwich.

Bolo is confused. "Coach Mark, will the kits have our names on the back?"

Coach Mark bites his lip and does not respond.

"I know my name," mutters Dazza.

Pellie groans. "Not again. We need a new kit to get names. A yellow one."

Stevie is reading his spider book.

He is unhappy because Dazza returned the other book for no

reason as soon as he arrived.

Coach Mark calls the team together.

Trundle FC have finished their warm-up and are having a final team talk.

Meerkats have not touched a ball yet.

Club photographer Joey Balley is waving from across the pitch.

Coach Mark gasps. Today was the day for the team's official photo.

Every Lane FC team gets one photoshoot a season.

The Meerkats' official picture was scheduled for today – when they don't have a strip.

Coach Mark looks to the car park. There is still no sign of Brendan, his parents, or the kits, which definitely do not have names on the back.

He trudges towards Joey, who has spiky hair and talks very quickly.

"All right Coach Mark, geezer man?"

Coach Mark likes Joey but never understands him.

Coach Mark nods, hoping this will be enough.

Joey continues: "I need to get your pocket rockets before the lens, Brother Mark! Like yesterday."

Coach Mark does not understand this either. He smiles again.

Joey grins back, waiting for an answer.

Coach Mark does not know what to

say.

The silence is awkward.

Coach Mark gambles.

"Picture? Now?"

Joey claps excitedly. This was obviously the correct reply.

Coach Mark looks at the team.

The Meerkats are not wearing their kit, but this does not seem to bother Joey, who is already organising them.

"Look happy! Get closer together and hug, like a rugby scrum."

Pellie's hand shoots up.

"We're playing football, not rugby."

Hildy, as always, agrees: "Yeah, we play football."

They don't move.

Coach Mark steps in and dishes out green training bibs to everyone, who quickly pull them on.

At least the team will be wearing matching tops.

Out of nowhere, Brendan appears.

Coach Mark breathes a sigh of relief.

"Brendan! You made it. Great. Where's the kit?"

Brendan shrugs and flicks a bogey.

"My dad brought me back. Mum still

can't find the tops. They think the birds have pinched them."

Coach Mark knows birds don't steal football tops.

He does not have time to point this out.

Joey claps again. "Right. Who is the star player?"

Dazza's hand shoots up. "Me."

Joey smiles, delighted to get a reply.

"Great, you two," he points at Dribbler and Bolo. "Lift this terrific player up, and I'll take the shot."

Dazza looks thrilled. No one else does. In fact, some are not even facing the right way.

This does not matter, apparently.

A second later, the picture is taken.

"Bravo, you were the best! What a team you dudes are! Laters!"

Camera swinging from his neck, Joey departs.

Without a kit and only one player smiling, the annual Meerkats U7s team photo is completed.

8. SECRET WEAPON

The game is due to start.

Thankfully Brendan's mum turned up with the kit – the bird theft story has been forgotten – and the Meerkats are now back in their blue strips with NO names on the back.

Apart from Pellie, who is wearing the yellow goalkeeper top.

Usually, Coach Mark would be worried about the team having no warm-up.

But today he has a secret weapon.

"Follow me, Meerkats."

Coach Mark does not wait for an answer. He marches towards the goal. The Meerkats look at each other. They know the team already.

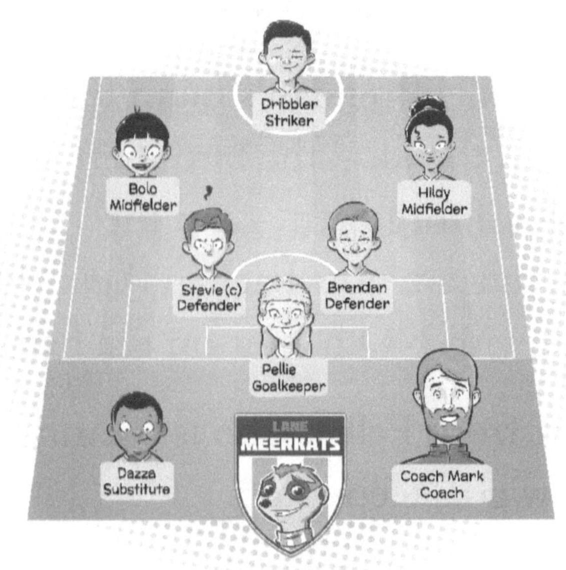

Coach Mark is being ODD.

He never does this.

One by one, they follow him. Even Stevie, still holding his book.

Today is weird.

Coach Mark has lost his mind.

He stops on the penalty spot and turns to the team who have followed him.

"Gang, today is different. We've had some heavy defeats and only Dazza has scored."

Dazza could burst with pride. Being the Meerkats' leading scorer is the best thing that has ever happened to him.

Coach Mark continues: "Something

happened this morning that changed everything."

Every single Meerkat is listening.

Pellie's hand goes up. "Are you feeling well, Coach Mark? You're not sounding normal."

To their astonishment, Coach Mark LAUGHS.

He says: "I feel great. We are getting better and it is time to prove it."

The Meerkats gawp at him. They know they're rubbish.

Pellie usually would ask another question but Coach Mark has become Crazy Man Coach Mark.

There's no point in asking Crazy Man Coach Mark anything.

Coach Mark continues: "We'll be great today. And the reason is … we have a secret weapon."

Having a secret weapon is AMAZING.

Meerkats have never had a secret weapon before.

"Catapults aren't allowed in football, Coach Mark," says Dribbler, suspiciously.

Coach Mark chuckles.

"No, it's not a catapult. Come closer."

The Meerkats huddle up.

"We are going to play well … because a gloriously huge spider is hanging in the goal behind me."

9. KICK-OFF

Everyone's eyes move to the goal behind Coach Mark.

Then one by one, they look at Stevie.

Trembling, Stevie drops his beloved book of spiders on the grass.

Hildy gasps.

Stevie wants to speak.

He opens his mouth but nothing is coming out.

Coach Mark's smile disappears.

Stevie does not look well.

"Breathe, Stevie, breathe."

Stevie's trembling is getting worse.

He is turning purple.

Dazza swears wisps of steam are leaving Stevie's ears. He is wobbling and looks like a kettle about to boil.

Pellie touches his arm: "Stevie. Say something."

Stevie is swallowing air.

The spider announcement is too much for him.

His mouth reminds Dazza of a fish. Dazza chooses not to tell Stevie this. Mouth open.

Closed.

Open.

Closed.

Finally, Stevie manages to spit out two words.

"Show … me."

Coach Mark carefully puts an arm around Stevie's shoulder as the team watches.

He guides Stevie towards the frame of the goal.

And points out the giant spider sitting in its web.

Stevie approaches.

Closer.

Closer.

Closer.

For one terrible moment, Brendan thinks Stevie may EAT the spider.

But then Stevie stops.

Trundle FC's players are moving on to the pitch, looking confused.

This is because the entire Meerkats team is standing in the goalmouth, with one player almost kissing the goalpost.

Meerkats ignore them.

They are watching Stevie.

Although some are looking at the spider too.

It's a scary-looking thing.

Suddenly Stevie turns around.

His face is red with excitement.

"Coach Mark. We have to call the game off."

"WHAT?" Hildy can't stop herself. "ARE YOU MAD?"

Coach Mark shakes his head.

"We can't call the game off, buddy," he says gently.

"Can't we move it and get on with the game?" Dribbler has noticed the other team staring at them.

Stevie is getting angrier.

"NO!

"We can't touch it."

Coach Mark smiles. He guessed the conversation might head in this direction.

"Well, that leaves one option then."

The team waits for the answer.

"We must stop the ball from coming near our goal."

Stevie's mouth scrunches up into a small ball.

"Leave it to me. I've got this."

Coach Mark pats Stevie on the back.

"They," he points to the Trundle players, "want to shoot at the spider. It's your job to save its life. Do you understand?"

Stevie says: "They won't touch our spider."

Stevie turns to the team.

"We do not let a goal in today. No matter what."

Stevie is sweating.

And they haven't kicked off yet.

Hildy claps with delight.

"Oh, goody. I love Angry Stevie."

The ref approaches, puzzled.

"Er, Coach Mark. Are you ready to kick off?"

Coach Mark studies the Meerkats.

This was the most unlikely warm-up ever.

Pellie's top is on back to front.

Coach Mark grins at the ref.

"We can't wait, ref.

"Our captain Stevie is ready for the coin toss."

10. SPIDER SAVIOUR

Stevie goes with the referee to meet the Trundle captain, shake hands, and do the coin toss.

Being captain is a great honour.

But Stevie does not look happy.

Coach Mark thought giving Stevie the captain's armband was clever.

However, as Stevie's foot paws the grass like an angry bull, he's now unsure.

After 30 seconds, the ref beckons Coach Mark over.

She says: "Coach Mark, we are waiting for your captain to call heads or tails, but he is growling and nothing else."

Coach Mark jogs over.

"Stevie, call 'heads' when the coin is flipped."

Stevie's eyes are locked on the Trundle FC captain, who looks petrified.

The ref tosses the coin.

"HEADS!"

The ref catches the coin.

"Correct. Which way would your team like to shoot?"

Stevie points towards the Trundle FC goal.

Coach Mark is relieved. Perhaps Stevie would make a good captain.

Stevie returns to join Brendan in defence.

Dazza is the substitute. He is unhappy, but his mum has bought muffins, an Easter egg and a chocolate bar, so he does not complain.

Coach Mark frowns at the sweets but

has other things to worry about.

The ref starts the game.

Stevie shouts at the top of his voice:
"ATTACK!"

And he charges straight for the
Trundle FC captain, who screams
and runs away.

Stevie ignores the ball and races after
the small boy.

Dribbler picks the ball up.

He beats one tackle.

And another.

And again.

It is a mazy run, weaving in and out of tackles.

He nearly collides with Stevie, who is still chasing the Trundle captain around the pitch.

Dribbler keeps going.

He's near the penalty area.

Parents gasp.

Coach Mark's heart begins to thump hard.

Is this it?

Can Meerkats score in the opening minute of the game?

Dribbler has dribbled around the entire team, apart from the goalkeeper.

He keeps going.

Around a defender for a second time and NUTMEGS a midfielder for a third time.

Then he flicks the ball over his head and races past another player.

This is INCREDIBLE.

The crowd applauds.

Dribbler is inside the penalty area with the goalkeeper approaching.

Hildy is alongside him.

"PASS!"

Everyone – except Stevie – shouts at Dribbler.

Confused, Dribbler stops.

In the last game, Coach Mark shouted that and when Dribbler passed to him, Coach Mark was angry.

He would not make the same mistake again.

He looks up.

And makes the pass … towards Pellie, back in the Meerkats' goal.

"NOOOOOOO!"

No one can believe how muppish Dribbler is.

Muppish is not even a word.

Check the dictionary.

See?

But muppish is the only non-word to describe how silly Dribbler is.

Every week Dribbler is dippier than the week before.

The ball rockets out of the Trundle half, slows down and stops.

Dribbler collapses with exhaustion.

Everyone waits for Pellie to charge out and clear the ball to safety.

Nope.

Pellie remains in goal. No one knows why.

"GET BACK!"

Coach Mark yells as the team stands and watches.

Two Trundle forwards begin running – fast.

This is ridiculous.

In a second, Meerkats have gone from being about to score to somehow conceding the first goal.

And Trundle FC have not even touched the ball.

Aware of the sudden danger to the spider, Stevie stops chasing the Trundle captain.

He begins running back to the Meerkats' goal – and the precious spider's web – as quickly as he can.

But no one matches Hildy for pace.

Years of ballet have made her legs quick.

In a few strides, Hildy overtakes everyone except for one of the Trundle strikers.

He hears her coming and sneaks a look behind.

Big mistake.

Hildy sweeps by him and knocks the ball back to Pellie.

The crowd applauds.

Coach Mark is stunned.

"That is BRILLIANT, Hildy!"

He gives a thumbs-up.

Hildy bows.

Coach Mark thought Meerkats had a chance in this game.

And he was right.

The first minute has confirmed it. They look quicker and more skilful than Trundle.

This could be it.

Meerkats' big chance is now. They can win this game.

And then Pellie – who is clapping Hildy's skill – lets the ball roll under her foot.

DISASTER.

The ball trickles towards the goal.

Parents gasp.

Pellie is not going to recover.

The ball is going in … without Trundle even touching the ball.

It reaches the line.

But does not cross it.

Out of nowhere, Stevie slides in and clears the ball for a corner.

The Trundle parents groan with disappointment.

The Meerkats crowd goes wild.

Stevie gets up, carefully avoiding the web.

He stands on the post, completely ignoring the back-slaps from the rest of the team.

Whenever a Trundle player comes close, the Meerkats captain growls threateningly.

They soon decide not to stand near Growling Boy.

The corner is weak.

Pellie throws herself on the ball. The crowd cheer.

Stevie shouts loudly.

"YES!

"Pellie, yes!

"No goals going in today!"

11. HELP

Coach Mark is standing on the touchline, super impressed with his team.

It is a terrible game.

Barely any passes and lots of violent tackling.

Yet Meerkats are not losing.

And it's nearly half-time.

This is incredible.

Dazza is the sub again. He's played for six minutes and then claimed to have a thigh injury.

However today it's not a problem.

Stevie is doing enough work for

three players.

And Hildy – who loves Angry Stevie – is doing the same. Those two have done almost all of the bad tackles so far.

And definitely all the growling.

Trundle has not had a shot on target.

And they've lost their captain.

After five minutes of being chased, the terrified little fella asked to leave the pitch and has not been seen since.

Coach Mark has also heard Stevie bark several times.

A few parents and the Trundle coach have asked Coach Mark if Stevie is well enough to play.

Coach Mark smiled and said nothing.

He's unsure where the strange dog-like behaviour has come from.

But he is certain of one thing – Stevie and the others would never have played so well without the spider.

The spider has been a masterstroke.

When they found the spider, he knew Stevie would do anything to protect it.

Nothing was getting close to that goal.

Coach Mark frowns.

Wait.

"Oh no," he mutters to himself.

At half-time, the teams will swap

around.

That means Meerkats will be kicking TOWARDS the spider and its web.

The spider that Stevie will do anything to protect.

That is the most important thing to Stevie.

Perhaps even more important than his book.

He will be trying to stop Meerkats next half, not helping them.

This is EXTREMELY BAD.

Coach Mark thinks hard.

The referee blows for half-time.

The Meerkats' parents celebrate. They've gone 30 minutes of football without conceding a goal.

Some are hugging. Others clap.

The Meerkats amble off the pitch, looking pleased.

Coach Mark fist-bumps each player as they come off the pitch.

Except one.

Stevie is sitting down on the penalty spot. He is looking at the goal with his back to everyone else.

Coach Mark sighs.

This is tricky. Football teams ALWAYS swap around at half-time.

He can't change that.

Stevie won't understand.

It does not matter what he says.

"Coach?"

Coach Mark realises he's daydreaming.

When he turns around at the sound of Hildy's voice, the team is looking at him.

Coach Mark says: "Gang, you've been brilliant. I am loving this."

The team likes Coach Mark being happy.

Hildy smiles extra wide – she thinks Happy Coach Mark and Angry Stevie are the best.

Coach Mark continues: "You can do this. When we change ends…."

Coach Mark stops talking.

He's got it. He has a new plan. He knows what to do.

The Meerkats look at Coach Mark, expecting him to finish the sentence.

No chance. Coach Mark delves into the football bag.

His bum wiggles like it's doing a tap dance.

They laugh. Coach Mark can be funny sometimes.

Eventually, he pulls a phone out of the bag. "Got it!"

He almost has tears in his eyes.

Coach Mark does not speak any more. Or look at Stevie.

He flicks through the phonebook.

Coach Mark needs to ask for a favour.

Because there is only one person who can save Meerkats from disaster. And the most unlikely person in the world will have to help them.

12. PEACE

JP, coach of the Under 15s Panthers team, is not happy.

He is inside Lane FC's equipment locker, untangling goal nets.

His phone rings.

JP fishes it out of his pocket and sees Coach Mark's name on the screen.

JP frowns.

He does not like Coach Mark or his team of weasels, meerkats, rats, or whatever.

He can still taste the wee from the last time he crossed paths with those horrible kids.

He answers the call.

"Yes?"

There is no hello or warm welcome.

Coach Mark says: "JP, I need your help."

JP replies: "No."

JP does not want to help Coach Mark.

Coach Mark is ready for this answer.

He repeats: "We need some help."

JP snorts: "No."

Coach Mark tries again: "It's important. But we have to do it now."

"No."

Coach Mark has one last try.

"It will help the club's café sell many teas and coffees."

JP pauses.

The club café NEVER sells much of anything.

Mainly because the tea tastes like pond water and the coffee smells like old sprouts.

This is interesting.

No one ever suggests they can help the café sell more.

JP does not want to help Coach Mark, but the club could buy new nets with the money.

He is torn. Through gritted teeth, JP says: "I'm listening."

Coach Mark punches the air.

He's won.

He whispers into the phone.

"Great. This is what we need you to do."

**

Half-time is over.

Stevie remains by the goal, ensuring no one approaches Stavros the Spider, whom he has named.

Trundle FC's players are heading towards Stevie, although Trundle's captain is still missing.

The Meerkats – minus Stevie – are lazing around, drinking from their water bottles.

Coach Mark is feeling nervous.

When the Trundle goalkeeper tries to stand in the goalmouth, he does not know what Stevie will do.

There is a strong chance it will not be good.

Coach Mark claps: "Right, team! Please do exactly the same. We go again."

Everyone staggers to their feet, except for Dazza.

He's holding his shin in pain.

"I've hurt my hamstring with my high-speed running."

Coach Mark suspects Dazza has no idea what a hamstring is.

He does not say this. Instead, Coach Mark nods.

"OK, everyone you know your positions. Dazza will be sub as he's … injured."

Hildy's hand shoots up.

Coach Mark's heart sinks.

"Yes?" What about Stevie?"

Coach Mark goes to reply but, as he opens his mouth, a loud siren interrupts him.

Everybody – even Stevie – looks towards the clubhouse.

JP is standing in front of the building, waving.

In a booming voice, he says: "Everyone. Please leave the field immediately.

"Our emergency meeting point is next to the café."

Everyone looks confused.

Someone in the crowd shouts back: "Why have we got to leave?"

JP holds his hands out.

"Do. Not. Panic.

"We have to evacuate the field … because there's a LEOPARD on the loose."

13. LOOSE LEOPARD

People scream.

Some run.

It is chaos.

Everyone rushes for the small gap in the hedge towards the clubhouse.

The match is forgotten.

But after a couple of minutes and no sign of a leopard, everyone calms down.

Parents and kids wait around the café with JP telling everyone that drinks are half-price.

The queue for the world's worst café is like a giant snake.

Coach Mark is baffled.

He'd asked JP to pretend it was a fire drill.

Why would he make up such a ridiculous lie?

A leopard?

Here?

JP is clearly insane.

Although looking at the empty pitch, the lie had worked.

With the hedge hiding the pitch, no one would see the next part of Coach Mark's plan.

Coach Maff, who sometimes helps Coach Mark, is with him.

The only other person there is – of course – Stevie, who is watching the bushes on high alert.

Coach Mark approaches Stevie.

"Er, Stevie? Are you OK?"

Stevie squints at the hedge.

"This leopard won't hurt our spider."

Coach Mark is unsure when Stavros the Spider became the unofficial team mascot.

Coach Mark clicks his fingers.

Suddenly, the leopard lie seems to be a really good idea.

He says: "Stevie. The leopard is somewhere over there."

Coach Mark waves towards the bushes.

"Let's move the spider and the goal to the other end of the pitch. Then we know we can keep it safe."

Stevie frowns.

He is thinking.

Hard.

Slowly, he looks at Coach Mark.

And nods.

"Yes, let's do it."

The three of them – Coach Mark, Coach Maff and Stevie – carefully lift the goal to the far end of the pitch.

They look a funny sight. Stevie has his hands stretched out as he runs alongside the moving goal.

He's planning to catch the spider if it falls off, but it doesn't.

They move the goal and gently place it down to the far end of the pitch.

They've done it.

Coach Mark nods to Coach Maff.

They grab the other goal – the one without the spider – and take it to the opposite end.

Stevie sits below the spider again.

For once, he looks … happy.

Coach Mark knows how he feels.

Stevie is fine.

The Meerkats are not losing.

Everything is good.

As long as the imaginary leopard doesn't show up and ruin everything.

14. SECOND HALF

"Why did you say that?"

JP shrugs: "What's the problem? It worked."

Coach Mark pauses.

JP is right. It did work.

But why tell everyone a LEOPARD is on the loose?

JP pats him on the back.

"Happy to help, Coach Mark. I hope the Meerrats, oops, I mean Meerkats, do the best they can."

JP strides away.

Coach Mark shouts after JP: "Thank you."

JP waves an arm without looking back.

Coach Mark rolls his eyes.

Who lies about a leopard?

Luckily, no one has realised the goals have been switched.

Or that the escaped leopard story was a complete FIB.

Despite this, the Meerkats are happy.

Dribbler wants to get started.

Bolo and Brendan are relieved JP has gone.

Dazza is finishing off a cream cake.

Pellie and Hildy are thrilled.

Stevie has insisted he will play in goal for the second half to protect Stavros.

This means Pellie will play on the pitch.

And the girls are super EXCITED.

Bolo and Brendan have agreed to be defenders, so Pellie and Hildy can play together in midfield.

This is GREAT news.

They even have a pigeon dance routine if the Meerkats score.

No one expects to see this.

Coach Mark groans: "Spiders. A leopard. Pigeons. It is like a zoo here today."

The Meerkats kick off the second half.

Dribbler has the ball.

To everyone's amazement, he PASSES – without even being asked.

Backwards. To Hildy.

She takes a giant swipe with her right boot.

And misses it completely.

The ball rolls through the middle of the Meerkats defence.

No one moves.

They're all looking at the ball.

Apart from the Trundle captain, who has reappeared after discovering Stevie has become the goalkeeper.

He streaks through the middle, controls the ball, and bears down on the goal.

On Stevie.

On Stavros the Spider.

Stevie has NEVER been a goalkeeper before.

So he does something completely unexpected.

Stevie dashes out, screaming at the top of his voice.

"ARRGGGHHHHH!"

He is wild, red-faced with globs of spit flying.

The Trundle FC captain has never seen anything like it.

He freezes with fear.

Stevie crashes into him, head-first.

THWACK! He sends the Trundle FC captain – and the ball – flying.

And then retreats to the goal to ensure Stavros is fine.

"Nice work, Angry Stevie," shouts Hildy.

"Well done, Stevo," yells Pellie.

Dazza applauds. Brendan picks his nose. Bolo pulls one of his ears.

Dribbler sighs.

Stevie ignores them all.

"Throw in, Trundle," says the ref, wondering what on earth had just happened.

As a Trundle player grabs the ball, giant dog Bonnie appears.

Coach Mark groans. "Not again."

Bonnie is always gobbling up footballs and loves to steal the ball and be chased.

For once, Bonnie ignores the ball.

This shocks

EVERYONE.

Instead, she charges straight into the bushes and disappears.

Today is a strange day.
The throw-in is taken.

Pellie and Hildy hunt the ball together.

Bolo and Brendan follow.

It's like a flock of sheep attacking whatever comes their way.

Stevie stands in goal, scowling if anyone dares to come anywhere near him and Stavros.

Dazza is enjoying a milkshake.

He is too injured to play any more today.

Dribbler watches on.

He is nowhere near the ball and is bored.

This game is rubbish for a striker.

Trundle are attacking

All the play is around the Meerkats penalty area.

But the Meerkats mob – and Angry Stevie – are not letting them get close to the goal.

The ball is crossed from the right.

"MY BALL!" shouts Hildy.

She whacks the ball straight into Bolo's tummy.

"OOOOOOHHHH!"

Bolo goes down, howling in pain.

Hildy forgets the game and checks on Bolo.

"I'VE GOT IT," screams Pellie.

She smashes the ball straight into Hildy's face.

Hildy falls on top of Bolo.

"HILDY!"

Pellie drops to her knees to look after her buddy.

The ball is loose but nearby.

Brendan takes a wild swing to clear the danger.

He misses and falls on to the heap of Meerkats players.

Coach Mark cannot believe what he is watching.

This is RIDICULOUS even for the Meerkats.

Three Trundle players take the loose ball and race towards the goal, leaving the Meerkats behind.

Only Stevie – and Stavros the Spider – stand between Trundle and the game's first goal.

Stevie's hands curl into fists.

With a fearsome scream, he charges straight towards them.

The Trundle captain is STILL terrified of Stevie.

Desperate, Angry Stevie follows the ball.

He slides along the ground, even though Coach Mark says slide tackles are not allowed.

He does not care.

He must stop them.

The attacker with the ball sees Stevie charging and, in a panic, passes the ball away from the tackle.

The goal is empty.

The Trundle captain takes aim.

On his knees, Stevie gasps.

Stavros is in danger.

And they've beaten him.

Stevie cries out.

Despite all his efforts, Angry Stevie can't help the best little creature he's ever met.

The Trundle captain shoots.

The ball flies straight towards the top corner of the goal, and Stavros's web.

Stevie cannot look. It is over.

Neither can the others – apart from Dazza – because they're in a huge pile.

The ball zooms to the goal line.

Meerkats have lost again.

No one moves.

Apart from the blur of a blue shirt.

Dribbler has never made a tackle.

And definitely not a header.

Yet here he is, flying through the air.

SMACK!

The ball pings off Dribbler's forehead and flies past the post.

Stevie jumps with joy.

Stavros has been saved.

Dribbler groans as he bellyflops to the ground.

Coach Mark applauds with gusto.

"INCREDIBLE, DRIBBLER! WHAT A HEADER!"

The Trundle players can't believe it.

Their coach is shouting: "Quick! Take the corner!"

The Trundle captain picks up the ball, which has rolled next to the bushes.

He stops suddenly. A strange noise is coming from the hedge.

The leaves are shaking. Crazily.

And there's snarling too.

Stevie runs to protect Stavros.

The Trundle captain backs away slowly – and then flees.

As he does, Bonnie bursts from the bushes. "Grab the ball!"

Coach Mark has lost numerous match balls to Bonnie the giant dog.

No one listens. Because Bonnie is not interested in the ball.

She's running away from the leopard that jumps out of the bushes.

15. FOG DOOD

Coach Mark and the Meerkats are standing together.

He says: "You did it, team. Well done. We were unbeaten in a match. What a result."

Pellie's hand goes up.

"The game was cancelled, Coach Mark. How is that good?"

Coach Mark smiles: "Because we didn't lose."

The game was abandoned with the scoreline still goalless.

Hildy's hand is next to go up.

"Have they caught the leopard?"

Stevie scowls. That leopard nearly

hurt Stavros – the most important thing in the world.

Coach Mark nods.

"Yes. Apparently, the leopard – called Linus – is good friends with Bonnie. They were playing chase."

Bolo frowns.

"Did JP know this?"

Before Coach Mark can answer, another voice speaks.

"Of course I did!"

The Meerkats spin around.

JP is standing there, holding a plate of cakes.

He is smiling. This is not normal.

"Congratulations, Meerkats. Great

result."

He holds out the cakes. They look incredible.

"I know we haven't always been friends but I'd like that to change – despite everything that's happened."

His eyes fall on Bolo and Brendan for a second.

"I've made you all my speciality – fog dood cupcakes!"

The team cheers. This is brilliant.

They avoided defeat in a proper game of football.

Stevie's spider is safe.

Linus the leopard is best friends with Bonnie the dog.

And JP has made cakes to celebrate, even if the name does sound familiar.

Life does not get much better.

Hildy grabs the first one.

She gives it a sniff.

"It smells funny," she says.

JP is already walking away.

"Give me a real big bite. It's the only way to eat them!"

Dazza eats his whole.

Bolo chomps straight to the middle of his cake.

Brendan takes off the top half.

Hildy pulls a face. She doesn't trust this fella.

Dazza falls to the floor.

"URRGGGHHH!"

Brendan spits the remains of his cake out.

"EWWWWW!"

The Meerkats do NOT like these cakes.

JP looks back with an evil grin.

"Oh, silly me. Did I not mention that fog dood cakes are made of …

DOG FOOD? Now, we're even."

JP walks away, cackling.

The Meerkats desperately try to spit out the rest of the cakes.

They'll get JP back soon.

You can count on it.

THE END.

For now. The Meerkats will be back with another adventure soon.

ABOUT THE AUTHOR

Martin has advanced cystic fibrosis (CF) and lives with his wife, daughter and dog in the UK.

He writes children's books in his spare time while trying to stay away from football speculation and repeats of Top of the Pops.

His children's books include:

The Football Boy Wonder

The Demon Football Manager

The Magic Football Book

The Football Spy

The Football Superstar

The Football Girl Wonder

The Football Genius

The Football Boy Wonder Chronicles

The entire Charlie Fry Series is available via Amazon in paperback and Kindle today.

Follow Martin on:

Facebook
Facebook.com/footballboywonder

Instagram
@charliefrybooks

ABOUT THE ILLUSTRATOR

Philip Knibbs is an illustrator with a background in comic book artwork.

Based in Bedfordshire, he lives with his wife, two daughters, one dog, two cats, two rats, four foster squirrels and a giant African land snail.

You can keep up with what he's currently working on at
www.philbertz.com

COPYRIGHT